First Facts™

Materials

Rock

by Mary Firestone

Consultant:
Dr. Audrey C. Rule
Associate Professor of Curriculum and Instruction
State University of New York Oswego
Oswego, New York

Capstone
press
Mankato, Minnesota

First Facts is published by Capstone Press
151 Good Counsel Drive, P.O. Box 669, Mankato, Minnesota 56002
www.capstonepress.com

Library of Congress Cataloging-in-Publication Data
Firestone, Mary.
    Rock / by Mary Firestone.
    p. cm.—(First facts. Materials)
    Includes bibliographical references and index.
    Contents: Rock—What is rock?—Sedimentary rock—Igneous and metamorphic rocks—
Mining rock—Cutting and crushing rock—Stone floors—Many uses for rock—Amazing but
true!—Hands on: make sandstone.
    ISBN 0-7368-2651-3 (hardcover)
    1. Rocks—Juvenile literature. [1. Rocks.] I. Title. II. Series.
QE432.2.F53 2005
552—dc22   2003026413

Summary: Discusses features of rock including how it is manufactured and made into useful
    products we use everyday.

Editorial Credits
Christopher Harbo, editor; Jennifer Bergstrom, series designer; Molly Nei, book designer;
    Scott Thoms, photo researcher; Eric Kudalis, product planning editor

Photo Credits
Capstone Press/Gary Sundermeyer, front cover, 5, 6–7, 15, 18
Corbis/Bob Krist, 14; Jonathan Blair, 12–13
Folio Inc./John Coletti, 20
Getty Images Inc./Time Life Pictures/Dave Lees, 16–17
Houserstock/Dave G. Houser, 9
Laura N. Scott Imagery, 19
PhotoDisc, back cover, 1
Root Resources/Doug Sherman, 11; Mary A. Root, 10

1 2 3 4 5 6 09 08 07 06 05 04

Table of Contents

Rock

Sam and Jessica play a game of chess. The marble piece feels cool to Sam's fingertips. A fire in the stone fireplace warms the room. Sam's cup sits nearby on a sandstone coaster. Rock makes up many of the things people use.

6

What Is Rock?

Rocks are made of **minerals**. Minerals are solids found in nature. Quartz, salt, and copper are minerals. Minerals often have crystal shapes. Crystals have shiny flat sides or pointed ends. People use rocks to make many things.

Fun Fact!
Most jewels are minerals. They are cut to have crystal shapes.

Sedimentary Rock

Most **sedimentary rock** is made from broken rock, sand, or clay. These things form layers on the bottom of rivers, lakes, and oceans. Rock forms when the top layers of sediment press down on the bottom layers. Sandstone and limestone are sedimentary rocks.

! Fun Fact!
The Egyptian pyramids are made of limestone blocks. The pyramids have stood for more than 4,500 years.

sandstone

9

basalt

Igneous and Metamorphic Rocks

Igneous rock forms above or below ground. Igneous rock forms when melted rock called **magma** cools. Granite, basalt, and obsidian are igneous rocks.

10

Metamorphic rock forms deep inside the earth. It forms when rock is changed by heat and pressure. Slate and marble are metamorphic rocks.

slate

Mining Rock

Workers dig large holes to remove rock from the earth. Workers drill and blast rock from the sides and bottoms of these holes. Large pieces of rock are loaded onto trucks. The trucks take the rock to be cut or crushed.

 Fun Fact!
Pumice is a stone mined from lava. People use pumice stones to smooth rough skin.

13

Cutting and Crushing Rock

Workers cut rock into smaller pieces. They use saws with diamond-tipped blades. These blades can cut rock into slabs or blocks.

14

Workers use machines to crush rock. Crushed limestone and clay are heated to make **cement**. Cement is mixed with water and rock to make concrete.

16

Stone Floors

People use stone floors in many buildings. Stone lasts longer than most wood or other materials. Marble is sometimes used for museum floors. Different colors of marble are put together to make patterns.

Many Uses for Rock

Rock has many uses. People shape marble into statues. Blackboards and pool tables are made of slate.

Rock is also used for buildings. Granite is used in the bases and walls of buildings. Granite is a hard rock. It is strong and lasts a long time.

Crazy Horse Memorial in South Dakota is the world's largest rock sculpture. People began blasting granite from the mountainside in 1948. When completed, the Crazy Horse Memorial will be 641 feet (195 meters) long and 563 feet (172 meters) high.

Hands On: Make Sandstone

Sandstone is a sedimentary rock. It is made of tiny grains of quartz and feldspar. These grains are held together when the mineral water they are soaking in dries. The water leaves behind a crust of minerals that holds the sand grains together like glue. Try this activity to make your own sandstone block.

What You Need

ruler

sand

two foam cups

warm water

Epsom salts

spoon

coarse sandpaper

What You Do

1. Pour 1 inch (2.5 centimeters) of sand into a foam cup.
2. Pour 1 inch (2.5 centimeters) of water into the other cup. Slowly add Epsom salts to the water while stirring with a spoon. Add Epsom salts until no more salt will dissolve.
3. Pour the saltwater solution into the cup of sand. Stir the mixture well.
4. Let the sand dry in the cup for several days.
5. When the sand is dry, peel the foam cup away from the sand block.
6. Gently rub sandpaper along the sides and edges of your sand block to shape it into a cube or block shape.

Glossary

cement (suh-MENT)—a gray powder made from crushed limestone and clay

igneous rock (IG-nee-uhss ROK)—rock that forms when magma cools

magma (MAG-muh)—melted rock deep below earth's surface; magma that flows out of volcanoes is called lava.

metamorphic rock (met-uh-MOR-fik ROK)—rock that is changed by heat and pressure

mineral (MIN-ur-uhl)—a solid found in nature that is not made by people, animals, or plants; minerals can be found on earth's surface or underground.

sedimentary rock (sed-uh-MEN-tuh-ree ROK)—rock formed by layers of rocks, sand, or clay that have been pressed together

Read More

Oxlade, Chris. *Rock.* Materials, Materials, Materials. Chicago: Heinemann, 2002.

Rosinsky, Natalie M. *Rocks: Hard, Soft, Smooth, and Rough.* Amazing Science. Minneapolis: Picture Window Books, 2003.

Internet Sites

FactHound offers a safe, fun way to find Internet sites related to this book. All of the sites on FactHound have been researched by our staff.

Here's how:
1. Visit *www.facthound.com*
2. Type in this special code **0736826513** for age-appropriate sites. Or enter a search word related to this book for a more general search.
3. Click on the **Fetch It** button.

FactHound will fetch the best sites for you!

Index